CHOOSING THE RIGHT PATH

A CAREER GUIDE FOR TEENS AND YOUTH

By

Nick Imoru

Achievers Publishing
Calgary, Canada

CHOOSING THE RIGHT PATH: A CAREER GUIDE FOR TEENS AND YOUTH

ISBN: 978-1-989291-06-1

Published in Canada, by
Achievers Publishing

Canadian Cataloguing in Publication (CIP)
A Record of this Publication is available from the Library and Archives Canada (LAC).

For further information or permission, address:
Achievers Publishing
Calgary, Canada
E-mail: info@achieverspublishing.com
www.achieverspublishing.com

Printed in Canada for Achievers Publishing

CHOOSING THE RIGHT PATH

A CAREER GUIDE FOR TEENS AND YOUTH

Dedication

To my beloved daughter, Nelly Imoru, whose passion, energy, and dreams inspire me daily. May this book serve as a guiding light on your journey to discovering and fulfilling the incredible purpose God has designed for you.

And to all the amazing teens in the Teens Church of Winners Chapel International Calgary, Canada, this book is dedicated to you. You are the leaders of tomorrow, chosen by God to shine brightly in your generation. As you walk this path of life, may His wisdom guide your steps, His love surround you, and His Word light your way.

With love and faith in your bright futures.

Table of Contents

Contents

INTRODUCTION

Why Your Career Choice Matters

When you think about your future, your career choice may seem like just one decision among many. However, it's one of the most important decisions you will ever make, especially as a teen or young adult. Why? Because the career you choose will shape much of your life. In fact, over a third of your life will likely be spent working. This makes it essential to choose a career that aligns with your passions, abilities, and values—something that brings you joy and fulfillment.

Imagine waking up every day dreading your job. Unfortunately, this is the reality for many people. Studies have shown that a significant number of individuals are unhappy with their jobs. A staggering 63% of people report that they dislike their job, while 24% go so far as to say they hate it. That's nearly 90% of the working population feeling dissatisfied in their work! Only a small fraction, around 13%, report enjoying what they do. These are sobering statistics, especially when you consider that your career will take up such a large portion of your life.

Why is it that so many people are unhappy with their career choices? Often, it's because they did not take the time to thoughtfully consider what really mattered to them when they made their decisions. Some people are driven by external pressures—whether from society, family, or financial concerns—without reflecting on what would truly satisfy them. Others may have simply chosen a path that seemed convenient, without evaluating how it aligned with their personal interests, skills, and values.

The truth is, God designed each of us with unique abilities, interests, and talents that He wants us to use. Your career should not be just about making money or fulfilling someone else's expectations; it should also be about walking in your God-given purpose. When you align your career with your God-given strengths and passions, you are more likely to thrive, both personally and professionally.

The Importance of Choosing a Fulfilling Career

Choosing a career isn't a decision you make lightly. It requires careful thought, reflection, and planning. The choices you make now as a teen or young adult will have long-term implications for your happiness, financial stability, and sense of purpose in life. A fulfilling career goes beyond just earning a paycheck; it provides you with a sense of achievement and satisfaction.

A career that resonates with your passions and values can make you feel that your work matters. You'll wake up each day with a sense of purpose, knowing that you are doing something meaningful with your life. When you are passionate about your work, you are more likely to invest time and effort into it, which in turn can lead to greater success and personal fulfillment.

A fulfilling career also contributes to your emotional and mental well-being. Doing work that aligns with who you are can help you feel confident, empowered, and motivated to continue growing. In contrast, a job that doesn't excite you or that conflicts with your values can lead to frustration, burnout, and even depression. This is why it is so important to carefully consider your career path.

The Parable of the Talents

As Christians, we believe that God has given each of us unique gifts, talents, and resources to use for His glory. This is powerfully illustrated in the Parable of the Talents, found in Matthew 25:14-29. In this parable, Jesus tells the story of a man who entrusts his servants with different amounts of money, called talents, while he goes on a journey. To one servant, he gives five talents; to another, two talents; and to a third, one talent. The first two servants used their talents wisely, investing them and doubling their value, while the third servant hides his talent in the ground out of fear.

When the master returns, he is pleased with the first two servants and rewards them for their faithfulness. However, the third servant is reprimanded for wasting the talent he was given. The lesson here is clear: God expects us to use the talents and gifts He has given us. Just like the servants in the parable, we are stewards of the abilities, skills, and opportunities that God has entrusted to us. How we use those talents matters—

not just for our own success, but for fulfilling God's purpose for our lives.

In the context of choosing a career, this parable teaches us that we must make wise decisions about how we use the gifts and abilities God has given us. A career choice is not just about personal gain; it's about honoring God by being faithful with the talents He has placed in our hands. Whether you have many talents or just a few, the important thing is how you use them to glorify God and bless others.

Choosing a career is one of the most important steps toward living a fulfilling life. It's not just about finding a job—it's about stepping into the purpose God has for you and using the unique talents and abilities He has entrusted to you. As you move through this book, you'll discover how to make wise and informed career decisions by considering five key factors: your interests, talents, skills, values, and job outlook. By the end of this journey, you'll be better equipped to choose a career path that not only brings you joy but also aligns with your God-given potential.

CHAPTER 1: UNDERSTANDING INTERESTS

What Are Interests?

Interests are the activities, subjects, or things that capture your attention and bring you joy. They are the things that you naturally enjoy doing, without feeling like it's work or an obligation. Your interests can range from hobbies like playing sports, painting, or reading, to activities like helping others, solving puzzles, or working with technology.

For example, consider the story of King David from the Bible. David, before he became king, was a shepherd boy. He had a deep interest in tending sheep, protecting them from danger, and playing music on his harp while caring for them. His interests shaped his early life and eventually prepared him for the greater role God had for him—becoming a king and a leader. David's love for music also led him to write many of the Psalms, which are still read and sung by believers today.

Here are some examples of interests you might have:

- **Being Outdoors** – You enjoy nature, whether it's hiking, camping, or just spending time outside.
- **Art** – You find joy in drawing, painting, sculpting, or expressing yourself creatively.
- **Computers** – You love working with technology, whether it's coding, designing websites, or troubleshooting issues.
- **Helping People** – You enjoy being of service to others, whether it's through volunteering, teaching, or providing support.

Why Interests Matter

Your interests are more than just hobbies—they can be key indicators of what type of career will bring you long-term satisfaction. When your career aligns with your interests, work feels less like a chore and more like something you genuinely enjoy doing. This is why identifying your interests is one of the first steps in making a wise career choice.

In the Bible, we see the story of Joseph, who had a deep interest in understanding dreams and interpreting them. Joseph's ability to interpret dreams eventually opened doors for him to serve in Pharaoh's court, where he was able to save Egypt from famine (Genesis 41:15-16). His interests weren't just random—they were part of God's plan for his life.

Similarly, your interests can reveal the unique purpose God has for you. When you are engaged in activities you love, you are likely to put in more effort and attention, leading to better job satisfaction and performance. Imagine choosing a career that not only pays well but also allows you to do the things you love every day. You'll be more motivated, productive, and fulfilled in your work.

Colossians 3:23 (NKJV) – "*And whatever you do, do it heartily, as to the Lord and not to men.*" This scripture reminds us that we should find joy and purpose in the things we do, working with all our heart as though we are serving the Lord. When your interests align with your career, you are more likely to put your heart into your work.

Practical Activity: Reflecting on Personal Interests

Activity Goal: This activity is designed to help you reflect on your interests and see how they can guide your career choices.

Instructions:

1. Take a moment to list at least five activities or subjects that you truly enjoy. These could be things you do in your free time, hobbies, or things you look forward to doing.

   Example:

   - Playing sports
   - Drawing or painting
   - Solving puzzles or brainteasers
   - Playing musical instruments
   - Spending time with animals

2. Once you have your list, ask yourself the following questions:

   - What do these activities have in common?

- Do any of them relate to a potential career field? For example, if you enjoy working with animals, perhaps a career in veterinary medicine or animal care might interest you.
- Are there any of these interests that you could see yourself doing professionally for many years to come?

3. Now, think about how your interests align with your talents and skills, which we will discuss in the next chapter. For example, if you love drawing (interest), do you also have a natural talent for it? Or if you enjoy helping people, do you have good communication skills to support that interest?

Worksheet Example:

- My interests:
    1. ____________________
    2. ____________________
    3. ____________________
    4. ____________________
    5. ____________________
- What do these interests have in common?
    - ____________________
- Possible careers that match these interests:
    - ____________________

Understanding your interests is the first step toward choosing a career that will bring you joy and fulfillment. As you reflect on what activities or subjects you love, remember that God placed those desires in your heart for a reason. Your interests are not random; they are a part of the gifts and talents God has given you to fulfill His purpose for your life.

As you move through the next chapters, we'll explore how your interests, when combined with your talents, skills, and values, can help you make a wise and fulfilling career choice. Stay open to the idea that the things you love to do may be the very things that God wants you to pursue as a career.

CHAPTER 2: DISCOVERING YOUR TALENTS

What Are Talents?

Talents are the natural abilities that you are born with—the things you do effortlessly, without needing much instruction or practice. Unlike skills, which are learned through education and experience, talents are inherent and often recognized early in life. These God-given abilities make you unique, and they play a key role in shaping the career that's right for you.

Consider the story of Bezalel from the Bible. Bezalel was an artisan whom God specifically chose to lead the construction of the Tabernacle. God filled him with wisdom, understanding, and talent in all kinds of craftsmanship, including working with gold, silver, and bronze (Exodus 31:1-5). Bezalel's artistic talent was not just a hobby—it was part of his divine purpose, and he used it to glorify God by building a sacred place for worship.

Examples of Talents:

- **Artistic Talent** – You might have a natural gift for drawing, painting, or designing things.
- **Athletic Talent** – Perhaps you excel in sports, having quick reflexes or strong physical coordination.
- **Musical Talent** – Maybe you can play an instrument by ear or sing beautifully without formal training.
- **Leadership Talent** – You may find that people naturally look to you for guidance, and you can inspire and motivate others easily.

Why Talents Matter in Career Choices

Your talents are an important factor to consider when choosing a career because they can determine how successful and satisfied you will be in your job. When you align your career with your natural abilities, you will find it easier to excel and enjoy your work. Just as

Bezalel used his talents to create something of great significance, you, too, can use your talents to contribute meaningfully in your chosen field.

In the Bible, we also see the example of Joseph, who had the natural talent for interpreting dreams. His talent not only earned him favor with Pharaoh but also allowed him to save Egypt from a devastating famine (Genesis 41:15-16). Joseph's success was not solely based on what he learned, but on his God-given talent. Your natural abilities, when nurtured and used wisely, can lead you to a fulfilling career that glorifies God and benefits others.

When you choose a career that aligns with your talents, you are more likely to succeed because you are already starting with a strong foundation. Natural abilities can make it easier for you to learn and grow in your chosen field. For example, someone with a natural talent for problem-solving might find themselves excelling in engineering or business strategy. A person with artistic talent could thrive in careers like graphic design, fashion, or architecture.

Proverbs 18:16 (NKJV) – "*A man's gift makes room for him, and brings him before great men.*"

This scripture reminds us that the talents and gifts God has given us can open doors of opportunity. Your talents are valuable and can lead you to places of influence and success when used wisely.

Practical Activity: Identifying Your Unique Talents

Activity Goal: This activity is designed to help you discover your natural talents, which will be important when choosing a career.

Instructions:

1. Reflect on the things you do well without much effort. These are often the areas where your natural talents lie. For example, you may be naturally good at solving math problems, playing a musical instrument, or organizing events.

2. Consider asking those who know you well—your family members, teachers, or close friends—what they think your talents are. Sometimes, others can see your talents more clearly than you can.

3. Below is a set of questions to help you identify your talents. Take some time to write down your responses:

   - What activities do I excel at, even with minimal practice?

- What do people often compliment me on or ask for my help with?
- What kinds of tasks or activities do I enjoy doing because they come naturally to me?
- When I face challenges, are there areas where I consistently find solutions easily?

4. Write down at least three to five talents you believe you have. If you're unsure, think about the things that bring you joy or the tasks you seem to do better than others.

Example:

- I am talented at playing the piano without reading sheet music.
- I am naturally good at organizing groups of people for events.
- I can solve puzzles and think logically without much effort.

Worksheet Example:

- My talents:
    1. ______________________________
    2. ______________________________
    3. ______________________________
    4. ______________________________
    5. ______________________________

Once you've identified your talents, consider how they might apply to different careers. For instance, if you're talented at art, you might explore careers in graphic design, animation, or photography. If you have a natural talent for leadership, you might consider careers in management, politics, or teaching.

It's important to recognize that talents are gifts from God, meant to be nurtured and used for His glory. The Parable of the Talents (Matthew 25:14-30) reminds us that God expects us to use the gifts He has entrusted to us. Just as the servant who wisely invested his talents was rewarded, you, too, will find success and fulfillment when you use your talents for a purpose.

By discovering your unique talents, you are taking an important step toward choosing a career path that will bring you joy, success, and the ability to serve others. As you continue through this book, you'll learn how to combine your talents with other factors like skills, values, and job outlook to make a wise career choice.

CHAPTER 3: BUILDING SKILLS

What Are Skills?

Skills are abilities that you learn and develop over time through practice, education, or training. Unlike talents, which are natural, skills require intentional effort to acquire and refine. Skills allow you to perform tasks competently and efficiently, and they are crucial for success in any career.

The Bible gives us an example of someone who developed valuable skills—Daniel. In Daniel 1:17, we learnt that God gave Daniel and his friends knowledge and skill in all literature and wisdom. Through their studies and training, they developed skills that made them stand out in the king's court. These skills, combined with their God-given talents, allowed them to succeed in positions of influence.

Here are some examples of skills:

- **Driving** – The ability to operate a vehicle safely.
- **Organization** – The ability to plan, prioritize, and manage tasks efficiently.
- **Communication** – The ability to express ideas clearly, both verbally and in writing.

Skills are essential because they allow you to take your natural talents to the next level. For example, if you have a talent for drawing (a natural ability), you can develop skills in digital art software, graphic design, or animation to expand your career options.

Why Skills Are Important for a Career

While talents are a great foundation, skills are what allow you to apply your talents effectively in a professional setting. In many careers, you may need to develop a specific set of skills to be successful. For instance, a natural leader (talent) might need to develop strong communication and conflict-resolution skills to lead teams effectively. A person with an artistic talent may need to acquire technical skills to create digital artwork or work with new mediums.

The story of the Apostle Paul provides a good example of how developing skills can expand your opportunities. Paul was a tentmaker by trade (Acts 18:3), which was a skill he learned and perfected over time. His skill in tentmaking allowed him to support himself financially while he carried out his ministry work. Similarly, acquiring skills can give you the flexibility to pursue various career paths and create additional opportunities.

The Difference Between Talents and Skills:

- **Talents** are natural abilities you are born with. For example, you may be naturally good at playing an instrument.
- **Skills** are learned abilities that you acquire through effort and practice. For example, learning how to read sheet music or play complex musical pieces would be a skill that enhances your natural talent.

Developing new skills is important because it can open doors that were previously unavailable to you. If you only rely on your natural talents, you may find that your career options are limited. However, when you invest time in learning new skills, you expand your career possibilities and increase your chances of success.

Ecclesiastes 10:10 (NKJV) – "*If the ax is dull, and one does not sharpen the edge, then he must use more strength; but wisdom brings success.*"

This verse emphasizes the importance of sharpening your skills. A dull ax requires more effort to use, just like lack of skills make tasks harder. By developing your skills, you can work smarter and more efficiently, bringing success to your endeavors.

Practical Activity: Skill-Building Action Plan

Activity Goal: This activity is designed to help you identify the skills you currently have and the skills you want to develop to support your career goals.

Instructions:

1. **List Your Current Skills:** Start by thinking about the skills you already possess. These can be skills you've learned through school, hobbies, work, or life experiences. **Example:**
    - I know how to communicate effectively in both speaking and writing.
    - I can drive and follow road safety rules.
    - I'm good at organizing my time and prioritizing tasks.
2. **Identify the Skills You Need to Develop:** Next, think about the skills you might need for your future career. For example, if you want to pursue a career in graphic design, you may need to develop skills in using design software like Adobe Photoshop or Illustrator. **Example:**

- I want to improve my public speaking skills to feel more confident in presentations.
- I need to learn how to use Microsoft Excel to manage data effectively.
- I want to develop leadership skills to manage a team effectively.

3. **Create an Action Plan:** Once you've identified the skills you need to develop, create a plan for how you will acquire those skills. You can take online courses, attend workshops, or ask for mentorship from someone who is skilled in the area you want to improve.

Worksheet Example:

- **My Current Skills:**
    1. ______________________________
    2. ______________________________
    3. ______________________________
- **Skills I Need to Develop:**
    1. ______________________________
    2. ______________________________
    3. ______________________________
- **My Action Plan for Developing New Skills:**
    1. I will __________ by __________.
    2. I will __________ by __________.
    3. I will __________ by __________.

Building your skills is an ongoing process that continues throughout your life and career. As you grow and develop new skills, you will find that your confidence and ability to succeed in different career paths increase. It's important to remember that while talents are given, skills are developed through dedication and effort.

Just as Paul used his tentmaking skills to support his ministry, you can use your skills to create opportunities in your career. Whether you are learning new technologies, improving your communication, or developing your leadership abilities, each new skill you gain will bring you closer to a successful and fulfilling career.

In the next chapter, we'll explore how your values play an important role in guiding your career choices, helping you find work that aligns with who you are and what matters most to you.

CHAPTER 4: UNDERSTANDING VALUES

What Are Values?

Values are the deeply held beliefs and principles that guide your decisions, actions, and behaviors. They are what you consider most important in life, and they shape the way you interact with the world. Your values can influence everything from your relationships and lifestyle to your career choices. They are the foundation upon which you build your life's direction.

In the Bible, we see strong examples of values shaping the lives of individuals. One such example is Daniel. He valued his relationship with God above all else, even when faced with the threat of being thrown into the lion's den (Daniel 6:10). His commitment to prayer and obedience to God's commands demonstrated the strength of his values, which guided his every decision.

Some common values include:

- **Christian Faith** – A commitment to living in accordance with God's word and principles.
- **Honesty** – A desire to live truthfully and with integrity in all circumstances.
- **Family Time** – Valuing relationships with family and making time for them in your daily life.
- **Helping Others** – A passion for serving others and making a positive impact on society.
- **Loyalty** – Faithfulness to people, causes, or beliefs, even in difficult situations.

Your values are unique to you and may differ from others, but they are crucial in guiding you toward a career that aligns with who you are.

The Role of Values in Career Choices

Your values play a significant role in helping you choose a career path that will bring you long-term fulfillment and satisfaction. When your work aligns with your personal values, you will feel a sense of purpose and meaning. However, when your career conflicts with your values, it can lead to frustration, stress, and a lack of fulfillment, even if the job pays well or seems prestigious.

Take the example of Moses. He grew up in the Egyptian palace with wealth, privilege, and status, but when he realized that his values were aligned with his Hebrew people, he chose to leave behind his royal life and identify with them (Hebrews 11:24-26). Moses valued justice and compassion for his people, and these values drove him to fulfill his God-given purpose of leading the Israelites out of slavery.

Aligning your career with your values means making choices that reflect what truly matters to you. For instance:

- If you value **helping others**, you might be drawn to careers in healthcare, social work, or education.
- If you value **family time**, you might seek a career that offers work-life balance, allowing you to spend more time at home with your loved ones.

- If you value **honesty and integrity**, you might avoid industries or roles where you feel pressured to compromise your principles.

In the Bible, we also see Joseph, who consistently upheld his values of integrity, even when faced with difficult situations. He refused the advances of Potiphar's wife, choosing to honor God and his principles rather than succumbing to temptation (Genesis 39:7-12). Joseph's values guided his actions, and ultimately, he was rewarded with success and influence in Egypt.

Proverbs 3:5-6 (NKJV) – "*Trust in the Lord with all your heart, and lean not on your own understanding; in all your ways acknowledge Him, and He shall direct your paths.*"
This verse encourages us to trust in God and live according to His values, knowing that when we do, He will guide our paths—including our career choices.

When you pursue a career that aligns with your values, you are more likely to experience satisfaction and fulfillment. Your work becomes more than just a job; it becomes a reflection of who you are and what you believe in.

Practical Activity: Exploring Your Core Values

Activity Goal: This activity will help you reflect on your personal values and see how they can guide your career choices.

Instructions:

1. **Identify Your Core Values:** Start by reflecting on the things that matter most to you in life. Think about the principles and beliefs that guide your decisions. Here are some questions to help you:

    - What principles are non-negotiable in my life?
    - What do I care deeply about, even when no one else is watching?
    - When faced with difficult choices, what helps me make decisions?

    Examples of core values:

    - Integrity
    - Compassion
    - Hard work

- Family
- Justice

2. **Reflect on How These Values Apply to Your Career:** Once you have identified your values, consider how they might influence your career choices. For example, if you value honesty, you might avoid careers that require unethical practices. If you value helping others, you might pursue a role where you can make a direct impact on people's lives.

   Example Questions:

   - How can I find a career that aligns with my values?
   - Are there any careers that would conflict with my values?
   - What kind of work environment would allow me to live out my values every day?

3. **Write Down Your Top 3-5 Values:** Choose the values that are most important to you and write them down. Consider how each of these values might influence your career choice.

Worksheet Example:

- My top values:
  - ______________________
  - ______________________
  - ______________________
- Careers that align with these values: __________

Understanding your values is a critical step in choosing a career that will bring you long-term satisfaction and purpose. When you choose a career that aligns with your core values, you are more likely to feel fulfilled and stay motivated, even during challenging times.

Just as Daniel, Moses, and Joseph lived according to their values, you too can choose a career that reflects the things that matter most to you. Your values are a gift from God, guiding you toward a life of meaning and impact. As you continue to discover your interests, talents, and skills, keep your values at the forefront of your career decisions.

In the next chapter, we'll look at the importance of job outlook and how understanding the demand for certain careers can help you make wise, informed decisions about your future.

CHAPTER 5: CONSIDERING JOB OUTLOOK

What Is Job Outlook?

Job outlook refers to the projected demand and availability of certain occupations over a set period of time. It helps you understand whether a career field is growing, declining, or staying the same. The job outlook for a particular field is often measured by factors like the number of new jobs expected to be created, the stability of the industry, and how these jobs compare to others in terms of competition.

Having a clear understanding of job outlook can help you make wise career choices. By researching how certain fields are expected to grow or shrink, you can better plan your future and avoid industries that may face layoffs, low demand, or stagnant wages. Job outlook gives you insight into what fields are more likely to offer long-term stability and opportunities.

For example, consider how Joseph, in the Bible, wisely planned for the future based on his interpretation of Pharaoh's dreams about an upcoming famine (Genesis 41:29-30). He understood the outlook for the economy of Egypt and took steps to store grains during years of abundance to prepare for the years of scarcity. In the same way, understanding the job outlook of different careers can help you plan ahead and prepare for a stable and prosperous future.

Why Job Outlook Matters

Choosing a career isn't just about pursuing something that interests you or aligns with your values—it's also about making sure that the career you choose has long-term potential. Job outlook is an important consideration because it affects job stability, demand, and your earning potential.

Job Stability:

Job outlook gives you a sense of how secure a particular career is. Some fields are more stable than others, depending on the economy, technology, and social trends. For example, healthcare and technology fields often have strong job outlooks because there is consistent demand for these services. On the other hand, industries that rely heavily on manual labor or outdated technologies may have weaker job outlooks as automation and innovation change the landscape.

In the Bible, we see an example of someone who ensured stability for his future by planning ahead—Noah. God instructed Noah to build an ark to prepare for the flood (Genesis 6:13-14). Noah's decision to follow this instruction ensured that he and his family were secure when the floodwaters came. Similarly, understanding job outlook can help you prepare for a stable career, ensuring that you are in a field with opportunities for growth and longevity.

Demand:

Demand refers to how many jobs are available in a given career field. Careers with strong job outlooks are often in high demand, meaning that there are more job openings than people to fill them. This can give you an advantage when applying for jobs, as employers are actively seeking qualified candidates.

If a career is in high demand, you are more likely to find a job quickly and have options to choose from. For example, careers in technology, healthcare, and engineering often have high demands due to the growing needs in these industries.

Earning Potential:

Job outlook can also give you an idea of the earning potential in a given career. Occupations that are in high demands often come with competitive salaries because employers need to attract qualified candidates. Understanding job outlook helps you make informed decisions about the financial aspect of your career.

When you consider careers with a positive job outlook, you are more likely to find a position that offers good pay, job security, and growth opportunities. This doesn't mean you should choose a career solely for its earning potential, but it's important to be aware of how job outlook can affect your future financial stability.

Proverbs 21:5 (NKJV) – "*The plans of the diligent lead surely to plenty, but those of everyone who is hasty, surely to poverty.*" This verse reminds us of the importance of planning for the future. When you take the time to research job outlook and make informed career choices, you set yourself up for success and abundance.

Practical Activity: Researching Careers with Good Job Outlooks

Activity Goal: This activity will guide you through researching potential careers and understanding their job outlook, helping you make informed decisions about your future career path.

Instructions:

1. **Choose 3 Careers of Interest:**

   Start by thinking about three career fields that interest you. These could be fields related to your talents, interests, or values. If you're unsure, consider careers in growing industries such as technology, healthcare, engineering, or education.

   Example:

   - Software Developer
   - Registered Nurse
   - Mechanical Engineer

2. **Research the Job Outlook for Each Career:**

Use reliable sources such as government websites, career databases, or professional organizations to research the job outlook for each career. Look for information on the following:

- Expected job growth (Are jobs in this field expected to increase or decrease in the next 10 years?)
- Demand for workers (How many job openings are there in this field? Is it hard to find qualified workers?)
- Average salary (What is the average salary for this career? Does it have strong earning potential?)
- Job stability (Is this career expected to be stable, or is it affected by economic changes?)

3. **Write Down Your Findings:**

Create a simple chart or list that outlines your findings for each career. Use this information to compare the job outlook for the careers you are considering.

Example of Research Chart:

Career	Job Growth	Demand for Workers	Average Salary	Job Stability
Software Developer	Strong (22% growth)	High demand	$107,510 per year	Very Stable
Registered Nurse	Strong (15% growth)	High demand	$75,330 per year	Very Stable
Mechanical Engineer	Moderate (4% growth)	Moderate demand	$88,430 per year	Stable

4. **Reflect on Your Findings:**

   After completing your research, take some time to reflect on what you've learned. Ask yourself the following questions:

   - Which career has the strongest job outlook?
   - Does the demand for this career align with my personal and financial goals?
   - Is this career stable enough to offer long-term security?

- Am I willing to pursue additional education or training if necessary to enter this field?

Worksheet Example:

- **Career 1:** ______________________________
    - Job Growth: ______________________
    - Demand for Workers: ______________
    - Average Salary: ___________________
    - Job Stability: _____________________
- **Career 2:** ______________________________
    - Job Growth: ______________________
    - Demand for Workers: ______________
    - Average Salary: ___________________
    - Job Stability: _____________________
- **Career 3:** ______________________________
    - Job Growth: ______________________
    - Demand for Workers: ______________
    - Average Salary: ___________________
    - Job Stability: _____________________

Understanding job outlook is a vital part of making a wise career choice. By researching the demand, job growth, and earning potential for different careers, you can make informed decisions that set you up for long-term success. Just as Joseph, Noah, and other biblical figures planned for the future, you too can plan wisely by choosing a career that aligns with both your interests and the realities of the job market.

In the next chapter, we'll explore how to balance all the factors—interests, talents, skills, values, and job outlook—so that you can make a well-rounded and thoughtful career choice.

CHAPTER 6: TAKING A BALANCED APPROACH

The Five Key Factors

Choosing a career isn't about focusing on just one aspect of your life. It's about taking a balanced approach by considering multiple factors that will contribute to your long-term happiness, success, and fulfillment. The five key factors to consider when making a wise career choice are:

1. **Interests** – What activities or subjects capture your attention and bring you joy? When your career aligns with your interests, it feels less like work and more like something you love to do.

   Example: If you love helping people, you might enjoy a career in healthcare, social work, or education.

2. **Talents** – What are you naturally good at? Your God-given talents can guide you toward careers where you can excel and contribute meaningfully.

   Example: If you have a talent for leadership, you might be drawn to roles in management, politics, or ministry.

3. **Skills** – What skills have you developed through education, training, or experience? Your skills are important for ensuring that you have the practical abilities required to succeed in your chosen career.

   Example: If you've developed skills in organization and communication, you might thrive in administrative roles or project management.

4. **Values** – What principles and beliefs guide your life? When your career aligns with your core values, you are more likely to feel fulfilled and purposeful in your work.

Example: If you value honesty and integrity, you might avoid industries or careers that involve questionable ethical practices.

5. **Job Outlook** – What are the prospects for growth and stability in your chosen field? Understanding the job outlook ensures that you choose a career that offers long-term opportunities and financial security.

   Example: Careers in technology, healthcare, and engineering often have strong job outlooks because of increasing demand.

By taking all five factors into account, you can make a career choice that not only suits your personal preferences but also provides practical benefits like job stability and financial security. This balanced approach will help you avoid the frustration that can come from choosing a career based solely on one factor, like interests or salary.

How to Balance These Factors

While it's essential to consider each of the five factors, it's unlikely that any one career will perfectly match all of them. That's why it's important to take a balanced approach when evaluating potential careers. You'll need to weigh each factor according to your priorities and determine which ones are most important to you.

For example, you might find a career that aligns with your interests and talents but has a weaker job outlook. In this case, you may need to decide if you are willing to take the risk for the sake of doing something you love. On the other hand, if job stability is a top priority for you, you might choose a career with a strong job outlook, even if it doesn't align perfectly with your interests or talents.

In the Bible, we see the wisdom of taking a balanced approach in the life of Nehemiah. Nehemiah was deeply passionate about rebuilding the walls of Jerusalem, and he had the leadership skills and commitment to make it happen. However, he didn't rush into the task blindly. Nehemiah took the time to assess the situation, plan carefully, and seek the king's support before beginning the work (Nehemiah 2:11-18). His balanced approach allowed him to succeed in completing the task, despite the challenges he faced.

When considering your career options, it's important to evaluate both personal satisfaction and practical considerations. Ask yourself:

- How important is it to me that my career aligns with my interests?
- Am I willing to compromise on salary if it means doing work that I love?
- Do I need job stability and security to feel fulfilled?
- How important is it to me that my career aligns with my values?

Proverbs 16:9 (NKJV) – "*A man's heart plans his way, but the Lord directs his steps.*"

This verse reminds us that while we plan and consider our options carefully, we must also trust that God will guide us toward the right path. By balancing the five factors and seeking God's direction, you can make a wise career choice that reflects His plan for your life.

Practical Activity: Creating a Career Decision Matrix

Activity Goal: This activity will help you create a clear, organized comparison of different career options by evaluating them based on the five key factors: interests, talents, skills, values, and job outlook.

Instructions:

1. **List 3-4 Career Options:**

   Start by choosing three to four career options that you are considering. These might be careers that align with your interests or careers you've researched for their job outlook.

   Example of Careers:

   - Graphic Designer
   - Nurse
   - Software Engineer
   - Teacher

2. **Create a Career Decision Matrix:**

   In the matrix, list your career options along the top row and the five key factors (interests, talents, skills, values, and job outlook) along the left-hand column. You will then evaluate each career by rating how well it meets each factor on a scale from 1 to 5 (1 being weak alignment, 5 being strong alignment).

Example of a Career Decision Matrix:

Factor	Graphic Designer	Nurse	Software Engineer	Teacher
Interests	5	3	4	5
Talents	5	4	4	5
Skills	3	5	4	4
Values	4	5	3	5
Job Outlook	3	5	5	4

3. **Evaluate Your Results:**

   Once you have filled in the matrix, review the total scores for each career. This will give you an overall sense of which career aligns best with the five factors. While no career may score a perfect 5 in every category, this matrix will help you see where certain careers may excel or fall short.

4. **Reflect on the Results:**

   After evaluating your career options using the matrix, take some time to reflect on the results. Which career scored the highest? Does this align with how you feel about each option?

   Remember that while the matrix is a helpful tool, it's also important to consider your intuition and personal preferences.

Worksheet Example:

Factor	Career 1	Career 2	Career 3
Interests			
Talents			
Skills			
Values			
Job Outlook			

Taking a balanced approach to your career choice ensures that you're considering all the important aspects of a fulfilling and sustainable career. While it's unlikely that any career will perfectly match all five factors, this approach allows you to weigh the pros and cons and make an informed decision based on what's most important to you.

As you continue on your journey to choosing a career, remember that God has given you the tools and wisdom to make a choice that aligns with your interests, talents, skills, values, and practical considerations like job outlook. By taking a balanced approach, you'll be well-prepared to step into a career that brings both satisfaction and success.

In the final chapter, we'll discuss how to confidently make a wise career choice, trusting in God's plan for your future.

CHAPTER 7: MAKING WISE CAREER CHOICES WITH CONFIDENCE

Using Biblical Wisdom in Career Selection

Making a wise career choice requires more than just looking at your interests, talents, and the job outlook—it requires wisdom. As Christians, we have access to biblical wisdom, which helps us make decisions that align with God's purpose for our lives. One powerful parable that speaks to the idea of using your gifts wisely is the Parable of the Talents (Matthew 25:14-30).

In the parable, a master gives three of his servants different amounts of talents (a form of currency) before going on a journey. To one servant, he gives five talents; to another, he gives two talents; and to the last servant, he gives one talent. The first two servants used their talents wisely, investing and doubling what they were given. However, the third servant, out of fear, buries his talent and returns it to the master without any increase.

When the master returns, he praises the two servants who wisely invested their talents and gives them greater responsibility. However, the third servant is reprimanded for not using his talent effectively. The message of this parable is clear: God has given each of us unique gifts, talents, and opportunities. He expects us to use them wisely, not to hide them out of fear or insecurity.

When it comes to choosing a career, we can apply the wisdom of this parable by:

- **Recognizing our talents** and using them in a way that brings glory to God and helps others.
- **Investing in our abilities** by developing skills and seeking opportunities to grow.
- **Not being afraid to take risks** or step out of our comfort zones when pursuing a career that aligns with our God-given gifts.

Choosing a career isn't just about making a living—it's about fulfilling God's purpose for your life. As you consider your career options, ask yourself how you can use the talents God has given you to serve others and make a positive impact in the world.

James 1:5 (NKJV) – "*If any of you lacks wisdom, let him ask of God, who gives to all liberally and without reproach, and it will be given to him.*" This verse reminds us that God is ready to provide the wisdom we need when making important decisions, including career choices. You can approach your future with confidence, knowing that God will guide you every step of the way.

Developing a Long-Term Vision

Choosing a career is not just about what you want to do next year or even five years from now. It's about developing a long-term vision for your future. This means thinking about how your career can evolve and grow over time, and how it fits into the bigger picture of your life and faith journey.

In Proverbs 29:18 (KJV), we read, "*Where there is no vision, the people perish.*" Vision gives you direction and helps you stay focused on your goals, even when challenges arise. Without a clear sense of where you're going, it's easy to become discouraged or distracted.

When developing a long-term vision for your career, consider the following:

- **Where do you want to be in 10, 15, or even 20 years?** Think about what kind of work you want to be doing and what impact you hope to have.
- **What steps do you need to take to get there?** This might involve further education, developing specific skills, or gaining experience in certain roles.
- **How can you serve God through your career?** Your long-term career vision should include how you can use your talents and resources to honor God and bless others.

In the Bible, we see examples of people who developed long-term visions for their lives and careers. One such person is Joseph. Although Joseph faced numerous setbacks—being sold into slavery, wrongfully imprisoned, and forgotten by those he helped—he never lost sight of the vision that God had given him through his dreams. Eventually, Joseph rose to a position of power in Egypt, where he was able to save his family and countless others from famine (Genesis 41:37-45). His story reminds us that God's plan often takes time to unfold, but when we remain faithful and trust Him, the outcome is far greater than we can imagine.

As you develop your career vision, remember that it's okay if the path isn't always clear or if it takes time to achieve your goals. Trust that God is guiding your steps and be patient as He works out His plan for your life.

Practical Activity: Goal Setting for Your Career Path

Activity Goal: This activity will help you create a clear roadmap for your career, outlining the steps you need to take to achieve your long-term vision.

Instructions:

1. **Define Your Career Vision:**

   Start by imagining where you want to be in your career in the next 10-20 years. Don't worry if your vision isn't perfect—this is about giving yourself a direction to work toward.

   Questions to Ask Yourself:

   - What kind of work do I see myself doing in the future?
   - How do I want to use my talents and skills to serve others?
   - What kind of lifestyle do I want to have? (e.g., work-life balance, financial stability)

Example Vision:

In 10 years, I want to be working as a graphic designer, creating designs that inspire others. I hope to use my artistic talents to serve Christian organizations, helping them communicate their message through creative visuals.

2. **Set Short-Term and Long-Term Goals:**

   Now, break down your vision into smaller, achievable goals. These should include both short-term goals (things you can accomplish within the next year) and long-term goals (things that will take several years to achieve).

   Example Short-Term Goals:

   - Enroll in a graphic design course.
   - Build a portfolio of my design work.
   - Apply for internships or entry-level positions in design.

   Example Long-Term Goals:

   - Gain experience working with Christian organizations or nonprofits.

- Develop advanced skills in digital design software.
- Start my own design business or work as a senior designer for a faith-based organization.

3. **Create an Action Plan:**

   For each goal, write down the specific steps you need to take to accomplish it. Include deadlines and resources you will need, such as educational programs, mentors, or work experience.

   Example Action Plan:

   - Enroll in an online graphic design course by [date].
   - Create 3 new design projects for my portfolio by [date].
   - Reach out to 5 design professionals for mentorship by [date].

4. **Review and Adjust Your Plan Regularly:**

   Life changes, and so do your goals. Review your career plan every six months or so to see if any adjustments are needed. Stay flexible, but keep your long-term vision in mind.

Worksheet Example:

- **My Career Vision:**

  In _________ years, I want to be working as _________, using my talents to _________.

- **My Short-Term Goals:**

  1. ______________________________
  2. ______________________________
  3. ______________________________

- **My Long-Term Goals:**

  1. ______________________________
  2. ______________________________
  3. ______________________________

- **My Action Plan:**

  1. ______________________________
  2. ______________________________
  3. ______________________________

Making a wise career choice involves more than just choosing the right field—it's about setting goals, trusting in God's plan, and using your talents to their fullest potential. With a balanced approach that considers your interests, talents, skills, values, and job outlook, you can make a career choice that brings both satisfaction and success.

Remember the Parable of the Talents and trust that God has given you everything you need to succeed. By developing a long-term vision and setting actionable goals, you'll be well-equipped to pursue a career that reflects God's purpose for your life. And most importantly, have confidence that as you seek His guidance, He will direct your steps and lead you to where you are meant to be.

CONCLUSION

Final Thoughts on Career Choices

As you come to the end of this journey, it's important to reflect on the key lessons learned about making wise career choices. The process of choosing a career is one of the most significant decisions you will make, and it requires careful thought, prayer, and reflection. Here are the main takeaways from this guide:

- **Interests Matter:** Choosing a career that aligns with your interests will make work more enjoyable and fulfilling. When you are passionate about what you do, you are more likely to put in the effort needed to succeed.
- **Talents Are Gifts from God:** Your natural talents are part of God's unique design for your life. Like the servants in the Parable of the Talents, you are called to use these gifts wisely

and invest them in meaningful work that brings glory to God and benefits others.

- **Skills Can Be Developed:** While talents come naturally, skills are learned and developed over time. By acquiring new skills and honing the ones you already have, you can increase your career opportunities and expand your potential.
- **Values Guide Your Path:** Your core values are the foundation of who you are. When you choose a career that aligns with your values, you are more likely to feel fulfilled and at peace with your work, even during difficult times.
- **Job Outlook Provides Stability:** While following your passion is important, understanding the job outlook of a particular career is equally crucial. A career that offers job stability, demand, and financial security will help you build a strong foundation for your future.

Remember, no single career will perfectly match all of these factors. But by taking a balanced approach and prayerfully considering each one, you can make a wise and informed decision that aligns with God's plan for your life.

Encouragement for the Future

As you move forward and begin the process of choosing your career path, know that you are not alone in this journey. God has a plan for your life, and He has equipped you with everything you need to succeed. The decisions you make today will shape your future, but you don't have to make them on your own. Seek wisdom, pray for guidance, and trust that God will lead you in the right direction.

In Jeremiah 29:11 (NKJV), the Lord says, *"For I know the thoughts that I think toward you, says the Lord, thoughts of peace and not of evil, to give you a future and a hope."* God's plan for you is good, and as you take steps towards your future, He will guide your path and give you the wisdom to make the right decisions.

As a teen or young adult, it's easy to feel uncertain about the future or pressured to follow a path that doesn't feel right for you. But take comfort in knowing that God has uniquely designed you for a purpose. Your talents, interests, values, and skills are all parts of His plan for your life. Trust in His timing, be patient with the process, and remain confident in the gifts He has given you.

Remember the lessons of the Parable of the Talents: use your gifts, develop your abilities, and don't be afraid to step out in faith. As you pursue a career that aligns with your God-given talents and values, you will find joy, satisfaction, and success. Most importantly, you will fulfill the purpose God has for you, bringing glory to Him in all that you do.

Philippians 1:6 (NKJV) – *"Being confident of this very thing, that He who has begun a good work in you will complete it until the day of Jesus Christ."* This verse is a reminder that God will continue to work in your life, shaping and guiding you as you walk in His purpose. He will not leave you on your own but will walk with you every step of the way.

As you look ahead to your future career, remember to stay focused on what matters most—your relationship with God, your values, and the gifts He has given you. Pursue a career that brings you joy, serves others, and honors God. And know that as you follow His lead, He will bring you into the fullness of the purpose He has for you.

ABOUT THE AUTHOR

Nick Imoru is a dynamic speaker, author, educator, entrepreneur, and consultant based in Canada. He is the President of Achievers Centre, a division of Philips Reliability Consult Inc. Nick's mission is centered on empowering the human spirit through consulting, coaching, connecting and circulating ideas and information. His goal is to inspire, ignite passion, create profit, and make a spiritual impact, ultimately helping individuals bridge the gap between where they are and where they aspire to be.

Nick holds a B.Eng. in Mechanical and Production Engineering and an MSc. in Advanced Technology from the UK. With over 18 years of experience in the Oil and Gas industry, he specializes in Maintenance & Reliability Engineering and is a Certified Maintenance & Reliability Professional (CMRP), reflecting his commitment to excellence in his field.

As the author of over 20 books and numerous articles and research papers, Nick's work spans personal development, spirituality, academia, business, and finance. He is the founder of Achievers Consult, Achievers Centre, and Achievers Publishing, all operating under Philips Reliability Consult Inc.

Nick is happily married to Dr. Margaret and is a proud father of two daughters, Nelly and Myra. His unwavering dedication to personal and professional growth, combined with his entrepreneurial spirit, continues to make a profound impact on individuals and organizations, guiding them towards success and fulfillment.

With a vision to inspire, train, develop, and unlock potential, Nick Imoru is committed to helping individuals and businesses achieve their highest levels of success.

To contact Nick or learn more about Achievers Centre, opportunities, speeches, and seminars, please use the information below:

Email: Nick@achieverscentre.com
Website: www.achieverscentre.com

BOOKS BY SAME AUTHOR

- A Heart for God
- Operating God's Private Lines
- Growing In Life
- Money & Pleasure: Trap of Purpose
- Success Buttons for Life & Academic Excellence
- The Making of Greatness
- Your Best Year Ever
- Nothing Just Happens
- How Did I Become Like This
- Achievers Daily Tonic
- Living in His Fullness: Unveiling the Life, Mission, Death and Triumph of Jesus
- Your Belief System: How Your Thoughts Dictate Your Life
- The Wit & Wisdom of Dr David Oyedepo
- The Tongue: How Your Words Shape Your Destiny
- Kings Don't Beg, They Make Decrees

- He Has Said...So We May Boldly Say
- Character: The Blueprint for a Great Future
- Living in His Light: Understanding Your New Identity in Christ
- Personal & Family Budgeting: Mastering Your Money for Financial Freedom
- Your Money, Your Future: A Student's Guide to Financial Success
- Choosing the Right Path: A Career Guide for Teens and Youth
- The 21 Life Rules Every Child Should Live By
- Saving Your Future: A Practical Guide to Financial Literacy
- The Power of Your Environment: How Your Surroundings Shape Your Life
- Think It, Do It: How to Turn Thoughts into Meaningful Action
- Adventures in God's Amazing Storybook, Part 1
- Adventures in God's Amazing Storybook, Part 2

To order any of these books, please visit:
Our online shop @ www.achieverscentre.com
or any of the amazon websites:
www.amazon.ca or www.amazon.com or www.amazon.co.uk, etc

www.ingramcontent.com/pod-product-compliance
Ingram Content Group UK Ltd.
Pitfield, Milton Keynes, MK11 3LW, UK
UKHW062254290726
14090UKWH00017B/692

9 781989 291061